Optimizing Relationships

Leveraging Habit Science for Deeper Connections

Horace Thomas Kennedy

Table of Contents

We are what we repeatedly do. Excellence, then,
is not an act, but a habit.

— Aristotle

Chapter 1. Introduction

In today's dynamic and fast-paced world, grounding our personal and professional relationships is paramount. The Special Report on the topic, "Optimizing Relationships: Leveraging Habit Science for Deeper Connections," provides an intriguing journey into the beautiful intersection of human connection and behavioral science. Without needing to wade through overly technical jargon, this report presents a trove of insights and practical strategies to help you harness habit science to enrich your relationships. Imagine enhancing your connections to the people you care about, your peers, clients, or even strangers you meet along life's path. This empowering, easy-to-understand resource can elevate your understanding of human behavior and transformation. Ready to take that vital step towards stronger, healthier, and more fulfilling relationships? Dive in and prepare to see relationship optimization in a whole new light!

Chapter 2. Understanding Relationships and Their Core Elements

We embark on our journey into the intricate world of relationships by first addressing their fundamentals, dissecting their core elements, and laying down the blueprint for our exploration ahead. Like a tree standing tall and sturdy, relationships are also grounded by roots - embodying certain paramount elements necessary for their growth and nourishment. These elements do not merely exist; they are consciously cultivated, tended, and imbued into the fabric of the connection between the individuals involved. They act as guiding forces, profound facilitators fostering deeper interactions, and solidifying bonds.

2.1. The Element of Trust

Trust, as a foundational element in any relationship, operates not just as a catalyst but acts significantly as the binding glue. Trust emerges from reliability, predictability, and consistencies showcased in mutual interactions. A simple analogy for this element could be thought of as the currency in a transactional world where anyone dealing without credibility would soon find themselves bankrupt of meaningful relationships.

The science of trust revolves around the release of the hormone Oxytocin. According to Paul Zak, a pioneering researcher in the field, Oxytocin enhances the empathy levels, making us interpret other people's intentions and emotions favorably. Thus, the virtuous cycle of trust amplification begins with the consistent release of this hormone in positive social interactions.

2.1.1. Building Trust in Relationships

With an understanding of the science, it becomes easier to consciously work towards building trust. Regular communication, transparency in behavior, predictability in responses, and dependability in actions are some of the key strategies to forge trust. It emphasizes providing consistency in actions, matching words to deeds, and building a track record of reliability that fosters trust.

2.2. The Role of Communication

Communication, often undervalued, sits at the crux of all human relationships. Quality communication is not about frequent interaction, but the depth of understanding, openness, respect, and empathy present. It provides a platform for both parties to express thoughts, needs, and concerns while fostering an environment of openness and acceptance.

2.2.1. The Science of Communication

Communication is ingrained in our biology. According to renowned anthropologist Robin Dunbar, language was developed by early humans as a form of social grooming that allowed us to bond with more individuals than bodily grooming alone. This bonding capability is crucial for constructing social structures of various sizes and intricacies.

2.2.2. Enhancing Communication in Relationships

Effective communication skills can be cultivated by employing strategies like active listening, where one deliberately focuses on the speaker, abstains from interruption and provides feedback only after the speaker has concluded. Practicing empathy, allowing room for feedback, and expressing oneself clearly and honestly, can also substantially magnify the efficacy of communication within relationships.

2.3. Acceptance: The Unsung Hero

Acceptance, often overlooked, plays a pivotal role in nourishing relationships. When acceptance exists, people feel seen, acknowledged, and valued for who they are. It eliminates judgment, fosters understanding and patience, contributing to a comfortable and genuine connection between individuals.

2.3.1. Acceptance in Practice

This critical element is practiced by genuinely observing, acknowledging, and appreciating the differences in the other person. It involves patience, understanding, allowing room for growth and shortcomings, and cultivation of the realization that we are all humans in flux and evolution.

In encapsulation, understanding the core elements of a relationship is the stepping stone towards creating stronger, healthier relationships. By employing and refining the elements discussed above - Trust, Communication, and Acceptance in our relationships, we set the groundwork for exploring how habit science can be incorporated to deepen these connections. You'll see these themes recurring and intertwining with the habit loops we'll discuss further. This cross-knowledge will prove insightful and intriguing, bleeding into practical strategies to cultivate habits conducive to enhancing the connections in your life.

Chapter 3. Diving into the Science of Habits

Commencing the exploration of this fascinating journey, we first delve into the fundamental principles behind habits and their formation. From the neurological underpinnings to the social and psychological factors affecting habit formation and crystallization, this segment offers a profound plunge into the science of habits. With an understanding of this, we can then start to see how these principles could be applied to relationship-building practices.

3.1. The Science Behind Habit Formation

Habits are ingrained and often unconscious patterns of behavior that are acquired through frequent repetition. From a neuroscience perspective, our brain experiences a fascinating process when habits are formed. Initial actions require conscious and cognitive effort involving the prefrontal cortex of the brain. However, as these actions are repeated, the neural pathways involved start to alter the fundamental architecture of our brains, making the action feel more automatic and less cognitively strenuous. This is essentially due to a central region of the brain known as the basal ganglia, which plays a crucial role.

The basal ganglia regulate habit formation by encoding and storing patterns of action-based outcomes. It rewards desirable behaviors, therefore encouraging their repetition, and punishes undesirable behaviors, reducing their instantiation. Essentially, habits are formed in the brain as a result of this reward-prejudice system, driven by dopamine-releasing neurons that signal pleasure or reinforcement. This neurotransmitter, dopamine, plays a pivotal role in habit development, fostering a reinforcement loop that strengthens the behavior making it more automatic and instantiated.

3.2. The Habit Loop: Cue, Routine, Reward

The underlying science of habit formation extends beyond the structural and chemical changes in the brain. The habit loop, a concept presented by Charles Duhigg in his book The Power of Habit, provides a psychological model that groups the process of habit formation into three stages: cue, routine, and reward.

The cue or trigger initiates the sequence. It can be a specific scenario, time of day, emotional state, or other sensory input that prompts the habitual behavior. The routine is the pattern of behavior that follows the cue. Subsequently, the reward, often a positive feeling or satisfying result, follows the routine. This reward reinforces the behavior, making the individual more likely to repeat the routine next time the cue presents itself.

3.3. Social Aspects of Habit Formation

While neurological and psychological aspects are crucial in understanding the formation of habits, the significance of the social environment cannot be underestimated. Social influences play a significant role in shaping and maintaining our habits. The interactions we have with others, the societal norms and expectations we encounter, and the environments in which we live significantly influence and mold our habitual behaviors.

Real-world examples can be found in numerous studies that showcase how peer behavior significantly impacts one's habit formation, with the effects being strongly prevalent in behaviors related to health practices, eating patterns, and even substance abuse. Essentially, the people we surround ourselves with can encourage the crystallization of certain habits and discourage others, playing a significant role in our behavioral development.

3.4. The Role of Self-Efficacy in Habit Formation

Self-efficacy, another essential element within the science of habits, refers to an individual's belief in their ability to execute behaviors necessary to achieve specific outcomes. Those who believe in their capability to instigate a change are more likely to adopt a new habit and sustain that change over time. Numerous studies have demonstrated that self-efficacy directly influences the process of habit formation, where increased self-efficacy can result in stronger habit development.

3.5. Conclusion: Habit Formation, A Multifaceted Phenomenon

In conclusion, habit formation emerges as a multifaceted phenomenon that involves a complex interplay between neurological, psychological, and environmental components. Understanding the science of habits primes us to understand how these ingrained behaviors can influence our interactions with others, hence setting the ground for our discussion on the intersection of habit science and relationship development in later segments. The mastery of this knowledge provides us a powerful tool to analyze and optimize our patterns of interactions, eventually leading to enhanced relationships.

Chapter 4. Interpreting Emotional Cues, and Why They Matter

Interpreting emotional cues, being one of the most dominant factors in any relationship, is essentially an exercise in human understanding and wisdom. Along with the subsequent interpretation and appropriate reaction, it is contingent on a myriad of neurological, cognitive, and social factors which we navigate on a daily basis. We embark on an exploration of this intricate process, bearing in mind its complexities, nuances, and uncharted markings. This chapter elucidates the connection between habit science and the art of understanding emotional cues, underscoring their importance in establishing and maintaining meaningful relationships.

4.1. Understanding Emotional Cues: An Introduction

A significant aspect of human interaction hinges on the interpretation of emotional cues. These cues can be verbal, such as tone, speed, and volume of speech; physical, as in body language and facial expressions; and even social, taking into account cultural background or personal past experiences. Emotional cues are, in essence, direct and indirect expressions of mental states which play a pivotal role in communicating desires, ideas, and feelings.

Making sense of these signals not only incorporates the decoding of the sender's emotional state but also the subsequent appropriate response, thereby impacting report and connection. Hence, enhancing emotional cue interpretation skills can fortify communication and understanding in relationships, fostering deeper connections and reducing misunderstandings.

4.2. Habit Science and Emotional Cue Interpretation

When delving into the world of habit creation, it is crucial to recognize the role of emotional cue recognition in forming meaningful habits. The process of habit formation, at its core, involves an action (or reaction) triggered by a cue, followed by a reward. In the context of relationships, these cues often take the form of emotional signals.

Understanding these signals and responding effectively can be nurtured into a habit, introducing predictability and stability into relationships. This involves consistent practice of suitable reactions to emotional signs, augmenting them with feedback, and rewarding the correct interpretations, resulting in a deeper emotional understanding.

4.3. The Importance of Emotion Recognition and Response

The adeptness to interpret emotional cues and respond appropriately has profound effects on relationships; it governs the effectiveness of communication, influences the perceived level of empathy, and facilitates deeper connections. Emotion recognition supports emotionally intelligent conversations which prompt healthy, constructive exchanges and discourage destructive, unproductive arguments.

Further, it enables us to demonstrate empathy— a powerful bonding tool that fosters understanding, acceptance, and appreciation. Lastly, it aids in resolving conflicts by allowing us to interpret the underlying emotional needs and respond effectively, contributing to mutually beneficial solutions.

4.4. Strategies for Enhancing Emotional Perception

Effective perception and interpretation of emotions can be enhanced through mindfulness exercises, active listening, empathy exercises, and cultivating emotional intelligence. Regularly practicing these approaches can nurture the habit of effective emotion recognition.

Mindfulness exercises encourage awareness and acceptance of one's emotions, assisting in recognizing those of others. Active listening promotes an in-depth understanding of verbal cues, fostering empathetic responses. Empathy exercises, like role-playing, can foster emotional understanding, and cultivating emotional intelligence can improve the interpretation of complex emotional cues.

4.5. Pitfalls in Emotional Cue Interpretation

The path to proficient emotional cue interpretation is not void of challenges. Individual differences, misinterpretation of cues, and emotional bias are common misconceptions that one needs to be wary of. For example, individual differences, such as cultural and personal experiences, can influence how one perceives and reacts to emotional signals. Misinterpretations may lead to unintended consequences, damaging relationships. Therefore, continually refining emotional interpretation skills is essential to avoid these pitfalls.

4.6. Conclusion and the Road Ahead

Recognizing and interpreting emotional cues form the bedrock of strong, healthy relationships. Harnessing habit science to cultivate the art of emotional perception and response is a powerful strategy for optimizing relationships. Although it's a journey laden with challenges - understanding individual differences, curbing misinterpretations, and overcoming emotional bias - the potential rewards of improving connections, communication, and empathy make it an endeavor well worth undertaking. As we forge ahead, it is important to carry these insights with us in our continuous quest for deeper and more satisfying relationships.

Chapter 5. Linking Habit Science and Relationship Management

Our journey begins with understanding the link between habit science and relationship management. The interplay between these two areas is complex yet fascinating. Habit science allows us to comprehend and design our behavioral patterns, while relationship management refers to the ways we connect and interact with others. By merging these fields, we unravel a side of human behavior often overlooked. Throughout this chapter, we will delve into how these two domains can overlap and function in unison to nurture and fortify our bonds with others.

5.1. The Confluence of Habit Science and Relationship Management

Habits, as defined primarily in behavioral science, are automatic behaviors or routines driven by contextual cues, summoned without conscious thought. It's like driving home from work and realizing, once you arrive, you hardly remember the journey. Your habits carried you through. Similarly, patterns of interacting and communicating in relationships can become habitual. Over time, we engage in these behaviors without conscious thought. Understanding the nature of habits can provide a pathway for shaping more effective relationship interactions.

Simultaneously, relationship management typically encompasses understanding, maintaining, and improving relationships in a personal or professional context. It addresses the dynamics between individuals in a connection, honing in on communication, mutual respect, empathy, and conflict management skills. Linking these two aspects can offer robust strategies for creating more satisfying and healthier relationships.

5.2. Unearthing Habits in Relationships

As we embark on this exploration of merging habit science with relationship management, we must begin by identifying the habits prevalent in our relationships. These habits could manifest in various behaviors, such as ways of responding to a loved one's emotions, habitual conflict resolution styles, or consistent patterns of demonstrating affection.

Identifying these habits involves introspection. Reflect on interactions with your partner, family members, friends, or colleagues. What patterns materialize consistently? Which recurring behaviors can you pinpoint? We propose keeping a habit journal, documenting your observations and insights daily. By documenting these automatic behaviors, we can gain clarity on the patterns we need to maintain or change.

5.3. Utilizing Habit Triggers for Relationship Enhancement

In habit science, every habit follows a structure, known as the habit loop: a cue triggers a routine, which then produces an outcome. The cue, or trigger, is the event that initiates the habit. Modifying our habits often involves identifying and altering these triggers.

In relationships, triggers could be emotions, words, actions, or situations. For instance, your partner's frown might trigger reassurance words from you, or the end of a workday might cue a check-in call to a family member. Understanding these cues and how they direct our relational behaviors can guide our interventions for habit change.

5.4. Formulating Effective Relationship Habits

Once we have exposed our habitual behaviors and their triggers, we can utilize this knowledge to formulate more effective relationship habits. Suppose you identify a tendency to react defensively to criticism from your partner. Your trigger might be the feeling of inadequacy, and the outcome is a defensive argument. Armed with this awareness, you can address the habit loop constructively: perhaps developing a habit of taking deep breaths when criticized (routine), eliminating the defensive argument (outcome).

Such intentional changes to your behavior patterns symbolize the core of linking habit science to relationship management. It takes persistence and practice, but the rewards are significant. Modifications to the way we interact can lead to improved communication, reduction in conflicts, enhanced mutual understanding, and, ultimately, stronger relationships.

5.5. Mapping Habit Changes to Relationship Management Strategies

Recognizing, changing, or forming habits isn't enough. You must map these behavioral changes to sound relationship management strategies. If the aim is to become more receptive to criticism, then this objective aligns with the broader skill of communication in relationship management. Deeper understanding of each other's feelings, improved conflict resolution strategies, and expressing appreciation more frequently could be other potential relationship management strategies driven by changed habits.

5.6. The Ongoing Journey of Habit Modification

The journey of intertwining habit science with relationship management is ongoing. The process of self-reflection, identifying triggers, changing routines, and mapping these changes to relationship-management strategies is repeated for various aspects of our interactions. This iterative cycle, when practiced consistently, can guide us towards developing relationships that are fulfilling, healthy, and marked by a deep understanding of one another.

Tying habit science with relationship management enhances our dimensional understanding of human relationships. It presents an empowering approach to transforming our interactions and connections with people who matter in our lives, ultimately enriching our experiences and opening a gateway to a myriad of possibilities for personal growth and stronger relationships. It is not a quick fix, but a meaningful and rewarding journey of discovery and transformation.

This chapter emphasizes the importance, complexity, and potential of linking habit science and relationship management. The next chapter, 'Effective Habit Development for Relationship Growth', will guide you through the process of intentionally developing new habits for relationship enhancement. For now, you've taken a crucial step towards understanding the interconnectedness of habit science and the relationships we cherish.

With this deep awareness, we're paving the way for healthier, stronger, and more satisfying relationships. We are evolving the way we connect with the world, one habit at a time. By understanding and embracing the intersection of habit science and relationship management, we're transforming the fabric of human connectivity—making our interactions more meaningful, fostering deeper connections, and nurturing relationships that not only survive but thrive in today's complex world.

As we continuously modify our habits, we witness a powerful shift in our relationships. So let us embark together on this transformative journey linking habit science and relationship management, weaving a tapestry of connections that are robust, resilient, and radiant with understanding.

Chapter 6. Effective Habit Development for Relationship Growth

In this segment of our journey, we delve into the fascinating dimension of effective habit development aimed at nurturing our relationships. It's a process which we'd like to think of as relationship growth gardening, a science and an art of planting, nurturing, pruning and harvesting habits to shape our relationships so they bloom into the lush, fulfilling and thriving entity they are meant to be.

6.1. The Role of Habit in Relationships

Habits serve as the invisible architecture of our daily lives, and have a monumental role in shaping outcomes including our relationships. More often than not, we are largely unaware of this intricate framework as it operates seamlessly in the background. Whether they are habits of communication, thought patterns, emotional responses, or behavior, they form a potent unseen force that carves the contours of our relationships. The ability to consciously recognize, adapt and shape these habits can be a tremendously empowering tool in our hands.

6.2. Habit Loop: Cue, Routine, and Reward

To apply habits effectively, understanding the fundamental mechanics of habits—the habit loop—is crucial. At its core, a habit consists of a cue that triggers a routine, leading to a reward. The cue is the trigger that initiates the habit, the routine is the behavior you automatically engage in as a response to the cue, and the reward is the positive reinforcement that the brain associates with the routine.

In essence, the mechanism governing the formation and perpetuation of habits is the dopamine-driven feedback loop. Whenever the brain experiences a reward (a positive experience), it releases dopamine, a neurotransmitter that induces pleasure. The brain is wired to seek repetition of this pleasure, thus motivating the brain to repeat the routine leading to that reward.

6.3. Identifying and Shaping Habitable Aspects of Relationship

The domains of relationships that can be optimally influenced by habits are vast and varied. These could range from habits of open and empathic communication, emotional response patterns, consistent actions that express love and gratitude, to mental practices that involve positive thinking and imagining. The key is to identify the existing habits in these domains, understand their impacts, and determine how they can be shaped, replaced or enhanced to promote a healthy relationship.

6.4. Framework for Developing Effective Habits for Relationship Growth

Developing effective habits for relationship growth can be done through a simple yet powerful four-step process: identification of cues and routines, substitution or enhancement of routines, and positive reinforcement.

+ Identifying the Cue and Routine: The first step is to be mindful and observe. Identify the cues that trigger non-productive or destructive routines in the relationship, as well as the routines that follow these cues.

+ Substitution or Enhancement of Routine: Once the cue and routine are identified, determine how the routine can be modified in a positive way. This could involve replacing negative routines with positive ones, or enhancing existing productive routines.

+ Positive Reinforcement: Positive reinforcement is key in sealing the new habit. The trick is to choose a reward that accompanies the new routine, giving your brain the satisfaction it craves. Over time, this would forge a new link in the habit loop, leading to the dissolution of the old habits and reinforcement of the new ones.

To further ease the process, a few tested strategies such as habit stacking (i.e., pairing new habits with existing ones) and shaping, which involves gradual modification of an existing habit, can be employed.

6.5. Overcoming Resistance: The Power of Visualization and Affirmation

When introducing new habits or altering existing ones, resistance can often rear its head. Fortunately, powerful psychological tools such as visualization and affirmation can be harnessed to overcome such resistance. Visualization is the structured practice of imagining the successful implementation of the new habit. The process of visualization essentially tricks the brain into shifting its established framework, thus facilitating habit change. Affirmations, on the other hand, are powerful positive statements that can rewire thought patterns, instilling confidence and motivation.

In conclusion, by understanding the science behind habits and harnessing it in a strategic manner, we can take control of the invisible levers that mold our relationships. Therein lies the power of conscious habit development for relationship growth, opening up a world of profound connections and transformative interpersonal experiences. This process isn't only about growing healthier relationships, but it also contributes to our own growth, helping us evolve into more responsive, compassionate and understanding human beings. Ultimately, it's a journey of personal evolution and self-discovery that influences and is influenced by our relationships. May this journey into your habit landscape be as illuminating as it is rewarding.

Chapter 7. Breaking Down Negative Relationship Patterns

In our quest to explore the all-too-important realm of relationships, it is incumbent upon us to navigate the often challenging terrain of negative relationship patterns. The ultimate goal of this endeavor is not to breed an atmosphere of blame or guilt but rather to use the illuminating light of understanding to illuminate the shadowed alcoves of our interpersonal interactions.

7.1. The Nature of Negative Patterns

To begin our journey, it is indispensable to comprehend the nature of these negative patterns. Quite often, they emerge as recurring ways of behaving, thinking, or feeling, which, over time, become entrenched in our relations with others. These patterns are counterproductive, causing strife, distance, and conflict in relationships. Their origins can be traced back to a multitude of sources such as past experiences, conditioning from childhood, or even biologically installed defense mechanisms. We sometimes hold onto these patterns out of a misplaced sense of comfort or familiarity, ignoring the destructive waves they continue to sow within our relationships.

7.2. Identification of Negative Relationship Patterns

The task of identifying these patterns is the first step towards their deconstruction. Tackling this step requires conscious reflection on our relationships and behaviors. The process may initially feel uncomfortable and challenging, as it necessitates sincere self-analysis and, in many instances, coming face-to-face with vulnerabilities and anxieties. Tools such as mindfulness exercises, journaling, or professional counseling can play a significant role in facilitating this stage of pattern recognition.

7.3. The Role of Emotional Intelligence in Comprehending Negative Patterns

Understanding negative patterns in a relationship is not merely about acknowledging our actions at a superficial level. Instead, it calls for a deeper dive into our emotional psyche. That's where Emotional Intelligence (EQ) comes into play. EQ is the ability to recognize, understand, and manage our own emotions as well as the emotions of others. A heightened EQ can help us unearth the emotional triggers and responses behind our negative patterns.

7.4. The Impact of Negative Patterns

Negative relationship patterns are deleterious not only for the health of our relationships but also for our overall well-being. Constantly existing in a state of conflict or emotional stress can lead to physical, psychological, and emotional health issues. These patterns, if left unaddressed, may instigate feelings of unhappiness, dissatisfaction, anxiety, and even precipitate the breakdown of relationships.

7.5. Strategies for Breaking Negative Relationship Patterns

The road to breaking these patterns oftentimes involves a commitment to self-improvement and change. This stage begins with acceptance and ownership of our patterns and their effects. While introspective understanding is important, taking action necessitates an empathetic stance, being open to feedback, and developing healthier coping mechanisms. Practises such as mediation, conflict resolution, or cognitive-behavioral therapy can be instrumental during this phase.

7.6. Overcoming Resistance to Change

Overcoming resistance to change is a cornerstone part of transforming negative patterns. We might find ourselves reluctant to modify patterns that we've clung to for years. Understanding that resistance is a normal part of the change process can bring solace. It's crucial to persist gently yet determinedly with changes, celebrating small victories and acknowledging inevitable setbacks.

7.7. The Potential for Positive Transformation

It is also important to remember that breaking down negative patterns isn't just about the elimination of the negative - it is equally about the birth of the positive. Each transformation unlocks the potential for positive aspects to flourish. Nourishing these positive behavioral patterns and fostering an environment of mutual respect and understanding can lead to healthier, richer relationships.

In conclusion, the process of breaking down negative relationship patterns is a road often fraught with discomfort and introspection. Yet, it holds the promise of realizing more fulfilling, deeper connections. Navigating this path, while challenging, is an endeavor well worth undertaking for anyone seeking to enhance their interpersonal relationships.

Chapter 8. Practical Strategies for Habitual Change in Interactions

Deepening and optimizing relationships hinge significantly on our habits, especially those that manifest during interactions. While habit science offers a wealth of knowledge about forming, maintaining, and changing habits, transferring such iconic behavioral changes into real-world context necessitates a practical, step-by-step approach. Hence, this section provides an in-depth analysis and description of practical strategies aimed at facilitating habitual change in interactions, ultimately to improve relationship quality.

8.1. Recognizing Habits Impacting Interactions

Before we delve into practical strategies for tweaking habits, we must first undertake the critical task of identifying the habits that predominantly influence our interactions with others. Just like the proverbial iceberg, a majority of our habits, especially those impacting our interpersonal exchanges, operate below the surface of conscious awareness. Often, these ingrained patterns of behavior will unleash their influence without us even knowing.

Why is identifying these habits so important? Because our habits — and most crucially, our awareness of them — set the tone for our communications with others, shaping not only our self-perception but how others perceive us. You might habitually cross your arms when you're engaged in a conversation, which could inadvertently signal defensiveness or lack of openness to others. The first step, hence, is to bring these 'interaction habits' into full consciousness, a process that requires consistent, sustained self-observation and introspection.

8.2. Framing Habits In The Context Of Interactions

The next step in leveraging habit science for relationship enhancement involves situating our habits within specific interaction contexts. This process allows for a more nuanced understanding of what triggers certain habits, how they manifest, and their resultant impacts. For instance, you might realize that you tend to interrupt others only in a group discussion, signifying a specific trigger and context.

In this phase, it's also important to evaluate the role of environmental cues. The Habit Loop model, a central concept in habit science introduced by Charles Duhigg, underscores the significance of 'cues' as triggers for automatic behavior or habit execution. Once you have a good grasp of the contexts and triggers associated with your interaction habits, you can then begin strategizing on practical ways to intervene.

8.3. Planning and Implementing Habitual Change

Understanding your habits is a great start, but translating this awareness into tangible behavioral shifts requires a well-structured plan. In this regard, implementation intentions, a concept pioneered by psychologist Peter Gollwitzer, can be extremely effective. This strategy involves crafting 'if-then' plans to delineate clear responses to specific situational cues. For instance, "If I am in a group discussion and feel the urge to interrupt someone, then I'll make a conscious effort to hold my thought and let them complete theirs."

Here, it's also worth enlisting the power of habit replacement, another valuable tactic elucidated by Duhigg. If breaking a habit appears too daunting, consider replacing it with a positive one. Following the earlier example, replacing the habit of interrupting with active listening can not only enhance your social competence but also enrich the quality of your relationships.

8.4. Evaluating Progress

Finally, the process of habitual change must encompass a system of consistent evaluation and feedback. This can include self-reflection, seeking constructive feedback from trusted others, or even professional guidance, if necessary. Remember that modifying deeply-entrenched interaction habits takes time and requires patience, persistence, and flexibility.

As we continually iterate and refine these strategies, we inch closer to mastering the art of leveraging habit science for habit change, consequently improving our interactions and relationships. By imparting practical insights into the mechanisms of habit change and providing actionable strategies for application, this comprehensive walk-through aims to empower you to take hold of the habits shaping your interactions and steer them towards healthier and more enriching relationship outcomes.

Chapter 9. Overcoming Challenges in Implementing Habitual Shifts

As we progress along our journey of understanding how to leverage the science of habits in the quest to optimize our relationships, it's clear that implementing substantial changes can often be met with formidable obstacles. In this expansive exploration, we delve deep into the challenges that people frequently confront whilst attempting to integrate new patterns of behaviour into their lives and interactions, and more importantly, how to most effectively overcome these challenges.

9.1. The Challenge of Change

Foremost among the challenges encountered when introducing habitual shifts is the inherent human resistance to change. We are, as a rule, creatures of comfort, often clinging to familiar patterns even when those patterns are ultimately detrimental. It is critical to bear in mind that altering habits does not simply require action; it necessitates an openness to breaking existing routines, and therein lies the crux of the challenge: the disquieting rupture of routine. Learning to remain steadfast in the face of possible upheaval is often the first, albeit intimidating, step in the process of transitioning to healthier habits.

9.2. Facing Fear and Uncertainty

Another significant challenge alongside change is the fear and uncertainty that it brings. By their very nature, new habits can seem uncharted and intimidating, often leading to a roadblock in our journey towards relationship enhancement. The key to navigating this roadblock lies in acknowledging our fears and uncertainties, remembering that these feelings are a natural part of the process. It is through recognition and acceptance of these fears that we acquire the strength to face them and, ultimately, rise above them.

9.3. Breaking Old Patterns

Making habitual shifts also requires breaking old patterns that have been ingrained over years, even decades. This challenge is particularly difficult when you're faced with negative relationship scenarios that are all too familiar – we react practically on instinct. The overriding challenge here arises from trying to break free from such patterns, and the solution is not so much about developing strength as it is about developing awareness. Being able to perceive when you're falling into old patterns and then consciously choosing to act differently is an empowering and transformative step forward.

9.4. Combatting Inertia

Inertia – the lack of motion or movement – signifies another demanding hurdle. A static state of affairs, whether in personal or professional relationships, can make the task of initiating meaningful habitual changes seem insurmountable. Inertia can be thought of as a comfort zone—stepping out is scary, but it's also the only path forward. Inertia is perhaps most pragmatically confronted by adopting an incremental approach to change, starting with small steps and gradually gaining momentum.

9.5. Dealing with Setbacks

Setbacks are an inevitable part of any journey, including ours. Encountering setbacks, and the accompanying disillusionment, can be disheartening, and can often lead to the abandonment of our purpose. Recognizing that setbacks are simply part of the process and implementing a resilient mindset can assist us in persisting even when we stumble, enabling us to learn from our mistakes and continue progressing.

9.6. Finding the Right Support

Lastly, having the appropriate support structure is key to overcoming challenges. Building habits that foster healthier relationships can be a steep hill to climb, but one that's much easier when you don't have to do it alone. Having the right kind of support – be it from loved ones, professional counselors, or personal growth communities – can be indispensable for staying committed to the cause.

In conclusion, while the journey to habitual shifts that strengthen our relationships is ultimately ours to make, understanding the challenges one might face can provide a crucial roadmap to navigate this change. Integrating effective strategies for overcoming these challenges can equip us with the resilience, perseverance, and insights needed to successfully implement habitual shifts.

Chapter 10. Case Studies: Successful Relationship Optimization Through Habit Alteration

Introducing this specificity in a dynamic weave, the case studies not only throw light on varied scenarios but also invite readers to deliberately scrutinize and analyze the presented situations and findings. Each case study unravels the power of habit science in optimizing relationships while providing indispensable takeaways to readers in honing their skills and attitudes towards relationships, moving one to reflect on their own behaviors, and constructively use the principles of habit science for relationship remodeling.

10.1. Case Study: Developing Empathy Through Active Listening

The first case study discusses John, a highly influential figure in his professional sphere. However, John's relationships with his colleagues were troubled due to his inability to actively listen to others' perspectives, leading to frequent disagreements and workplace conflicts. As a solution, he introduced a small habitual change: he began to consciously paraphrase what others said before putting forth his own points. As a result, his coworkers felt more valued and understood, hence leading to improved relationships. The influence of this new habit expanded beyond John's professional life, seeping into his personal relationships as well as becoming an effective communicator.

10.2. Case Study: Adopting Habitual Affection to Strengthen Marital Bonds

We then delve into the life of Maria, a busy professional who had neglected her marital relationship, leading to escalating tensions between her and her spouse. She then tapped into the power of habit science to introduce micro-expressions of affection into her daily routine with her husband, such as a friendly touch, warm greetings, and sincere compliments. These small yet impactful habitual changes elicited a deeper sense of bonding, culminating in an ameliorated and enriched marital relationship.

10.3. Case Study: Building Trust Through Consistency in Parent-Child Relationship

Next, we explore the experience of Andrew, a father in a constant power struggle with his teenage daughter. Through adopting consistency in his actions and promises, Andrew was able to positively alter his relationship. He ensured that his words and actions were consistent, hence reinforcing his integrity in his daughter's eyes, leading to the enhanced trust and eased tensions in their relationship.

10.4. Case Study: Improving Teacher-Student Relationship Through Mindful Communication

Our fourth case study explores Mrs. Smith, a school teacher

struggling with the task of managing and connecting with her students. Taking note of the power of habit science, she decided to adopt a new method of communication. She started expressing her thoughts clearly and compassionately, encouraging her students to express their opinions and feelings. This improvement in communication habit leads to a better teacher-student relationship, fostering a nurturing learning environment.

10.5. Case Study: Enhancing Client Relationships Through Positive Reinforcements

Lastly, we examine the case of Sarah, a sales executive struggling with declining client relationships. A change in her habit introduced acknowledging clients' perspectives, appreciating their insights, and regularly following up with genuine courtesy, which acted as positive reinforcements. As she incorporated these habits, she noticed strengthened relationships with her clients - marking increased client satisfaction and retention.

The investigation of these different scenarios illuminates how the touch of habit alteration hints at transformation, improving relationships manifold. Each instance stands as a testament to the power of habit science in relationship optimization. The deliberate acknowledgment of behavioral patterns, understanding the core of the issue, initiating unique customized habitual change, and carving the journey towards a solution, all conjoin to form the beautiful mosaic of optimized and wholesome relationships.

These case studies offer valuable insights into the profound impact tiny habitual shifts can have on relationships. These tangible and relatable transformations not only provide a sense of optimism but also equip readers with practical methodologies that they can utilize in their respective circumstances. By presenting a multifaceted view on the employment of habit science for relationship optimization, it nudges academic as well as personal growth in readers, encouraging them to adapt, learn, and grow. It impressively draws the subtle thread connecting habit science and relationship management while also intriguing one's curiosity to dig deeper into this enlightening field.

Thus, dissecting these cases in detail, readers demystify the influence and working of habit science and are empowered to replicate the success stories in their lives to strive for happier, healthier, and more fulfilling relationships. It propels the readers to reassess their habitual patterns, remodel them constructively, and venture into the exciting journey of relationship optimization!

Chapter 11. Future Perspectives: Habit Science and Its Role in Relationship Enhancement

As we navigate the contours of the future, habit science will become an intrinsic part of our understanding and enhancement of relationships, both personal and professional. Progressing from the realms of theoretical inquiry into practical application, the science of habits will guide us in cultivating healthier interconnections, improved communication, and deeper understanding.

11.1. The Interplay of Habit Science and Relationships

The nexus of habit science and relationships is a fascinating dance between behavior patterns, emotional response and, ultimately, the depth of connections we form with one another. Habit science explores the repeated behaviors that, over time, form powerful bonds within our psyche. This science gives us valuable insight into our automatic actions and reactions. Translated into the sphere of relationships, this knowledge empowers us to purposefully shape and improve our communication patterns, enhance our understanding of others, and foster deeper connections.

11.2. The Application of Habit Science in Relationships

Habit science, when applied to relationships, allows for targeted transformation. From understanding the cues that spark our behavioral habits, to recognizing the satisfaction derived from repeated patterns, and the potential discomfort associated with breaking them, we are presented with a roadmap. This roadmap directs us towards healthier communication patterns, more satisfying interactions, and, ultimately, deeper connections with others.

Just as we condition ourselves into unhealthy patterns, we can also nurture healthy habits within our relationships. Using the science of habits, we can cultivate practices such as active listening, empathy, and open communication. Each of these elements are fabricated from smaller behaviors that, when consistently practiced, compound into larger relational enhancements.

11.3. Optimizing Relationships Through Habit Science

The future of relationships rests partly within the field of habit science. Harnessing its potential gives us a unique key to optimizing our connections. Battling habitual responses wired deep within us is no easy feat; it often entails unlearning years, possibly decades, of automatic responses. However, through consistent and conscious effort, change is achievable.

Our behaviors directly affect those around us. As we modify our patterns, we inspire ripples of transformation in our relationships. Even the slightest behavioral modification can lead to significant shifts in the dynamics of our interactions. For example, practicing empathy can lead to a more nurturing environment, while open, non-judgmental communication can minimize misunderstandings and foster stronger connections.

11.4. Case-In-Point: Successful Transformations

Transitional stages can be witnessed in various stories of success, where habit science has been effectively leveraged in relational enhancements. These profound transformations open up a vista of potential applications for habit science in transforming relationships. Personal tales of successful habit transformation could, in time, lend themselves to creating a comprehensive guide on employing habit science in relationship enhancement.

11.5. Approaching Challenges and Setbacks

Undeniably, the journey to optimizing relationships through habit science is not without challenges. It requires conscious effort, self-awareness, and patience. The natural resistance to change often results in initial setbacks. However, a holistic understanding of habit science equips us with the knowledge that change is a process, not an event. These challenges are integral parts of the journey towards healthier habits and improved relationships.

11.6. Conclusion: Looking Towards the Future

As we continue to delve deeper into the application of habit science to relationship enhancement, we must be prepared for the journey of transformation. This journey may be fraught with challenges and setbacks, but asseted with habit science, we have an empowering tool. This intersection of habit science and human relationships holds incredible potential for fostering communication, understanding, and connection.

The future of relationships, adorned with habit science, shapes up to be an era of awakened understanding and deeper connections. The realization that the quality of our lives is intricately connected to the quality of our relationships directs us towards harnessing habit science for relationship improvement. Thus, habit science does more than predicting our behavior; it equips us with the key to transform and strengthen our relationships in this dynamic world.

www.ingramcontent.com/pod-product-compliance
Lightning Source LLC
Chambersburg PA
CBHW061536250726
48657CB00005B/2255